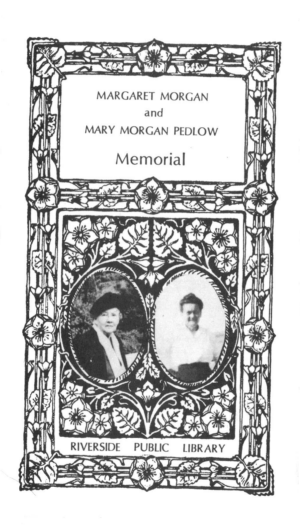

MARGARET MORGAN
and
MARY MORGAN PEDLOW

Memorial

RIVERSIDE PUBLIC LIBRARY

The INCREDIBLE JOURNEY to the DEPTHS of the OCEAN

Created and produced by Nicholas Harris, Joanna Turner
and Claire Aston, Orpheus Books Ltd

Illustrators Elisabetta Ferrero *(Milan Illustrations
Agency)*, Gary Hincks

Consultant Dr Brian Bett, marine biologist at
Southampton Oceanography Centre, England

Published in the United States in 2000 by
Peter Bedrick Books
A division of NTC/Contemporary Publishing Group, Inc.
4255 West Touhy Avenue,
Lincolnwood (Chicago), IL 60712-1975

Printed and bound in Singapore

International Standard Book Number: 0-87226-601-X

The INCREDIBLE
JOURNEY to the DEPTHS of the
OCEAN

Nicholas Harris

illustrated by
Elisabetta Ferrero
and Gary Hincks

PETER BEDRICK BOOKS
NTC/Contemporary Publishing Group
NEW YORK

CONTENTS

Great white shark

Coelacanth

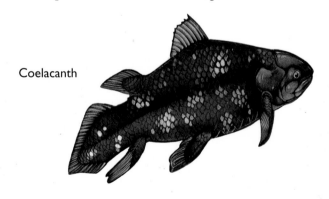

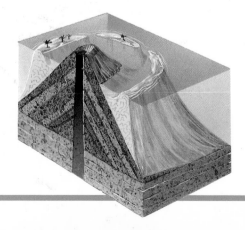

INTRODUCTION

OCEAN WATERS cover nearly three-quarters of our planet, yet until recently we knew very little about what lay beneath them—the nature of the ocean floor or what kinds of living things lurked deep below the ocean surface. In fact, people used to think that no animals could inhabit the deep-ocean waters. It would be too cold and dark; they would be crushed by the weight of the sea water above them; there would in any case be no food for them to eat.

Then, from the mid-1800s onwards, exciting discoveries were made. Extraordinary animals never seen before were hauled up from the depths. Scientists found ways of measuring the depth of the ocean floor using echo-sounding equipment (the same way that whales and dolphins communicate with one another). Traveling in submersibles, scientists could explore great depths.

As you will discover on the journey you are about to make, we now know that there is an amazing diversity of life found at all depths of the oceans. And sensational new finds are still being made *(see page 26)*. Even the huge megamouth shark was discovered only as recently as 1977.

Who knows what mysteries of the oceans will be revealed in future years?

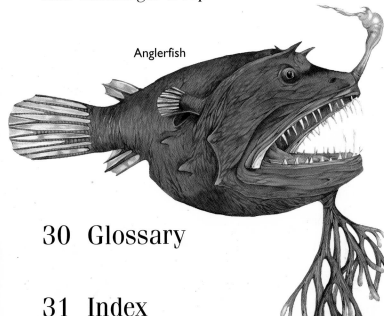

Anglerfish

Across the Ocean

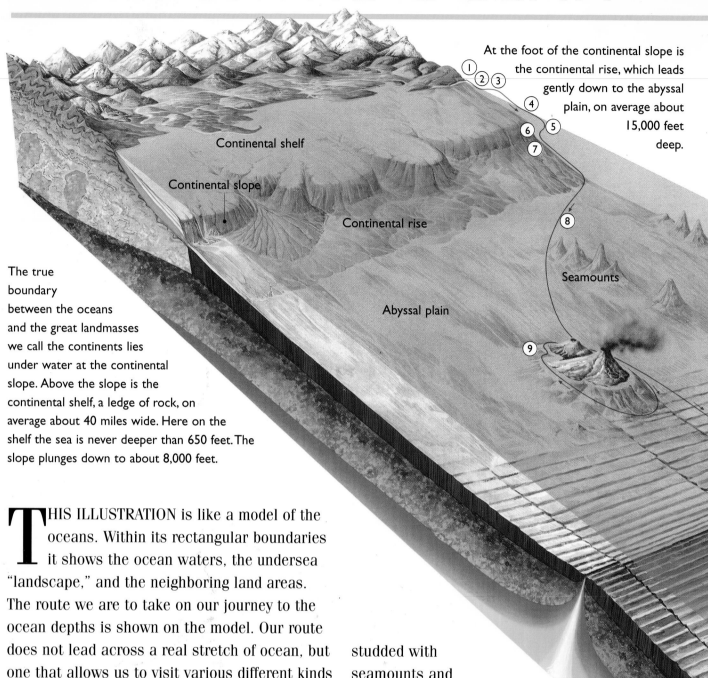

Continental shelf

Continental slope

Continental rise

At the foot of the continental slope is the continental rise, which leads gently down to the abyssal plain, on average about 15,000 feet deep.

① ② ③ ④ ⑤ ⑥ ⑦ ⑧ ⑨

Seamounts

Abyssal plain

The true boundary between the oceans and the great landmasses we call the continents lies under water at the continental slope. Above the slope is the continental shelf, a ledge of rock, on average about 40 miles wide. Here on the shelf the sea is never deeper than 650 feet. The slope plunges down to about 8,000 feet.

THIS ILLUSTRATION is like a model of the oceans. Within its rectangular boundaries it shows the ocean waters, the undersea "landscape," and the neighboring land areas. The route we are to take on our journey to the ocean depths is shown on the model. Our route does not lead across a real stretch of ocean, but one that allows us to visit various different kinds of ocean environment.

We begin at the seashore (1), where land meets sea. Just offshore, still in shallow water, lies a kelp forest (2), home to a rich variety of wildlife. Farther out to sea we watch the animals that live just above, or close to, the ocean surface (3), before plunging into the water itself (4). From there, we dive down through the deeper, barely-lit waters of the "twilight zone" (5) before meeting the strange creatures that inhabit the deep-water bathypelagic zone (6). We come to rest on the continental slope (7) before making our way down to the abyssal plain (8). The plain is studded with seamounts and underwater volcanoes. Some are tall enough to break the waters as oceanic islands. We climb one and explore the amazing variety of life that inhabits the shallow, warm waters of a coral reef (9).

Back on the abyssal plain, we slowly ascend the mid-oceanic ridge (10), actually a chain of volcanoes that winds across the ocean floor, and discover hydrothermal vents. Continuing across the abyssal plain, we suddenly plummet to more than twice our depth below the surface and reach our final destination—a deep-ocean trench (11), one of the deepest points on Earth.

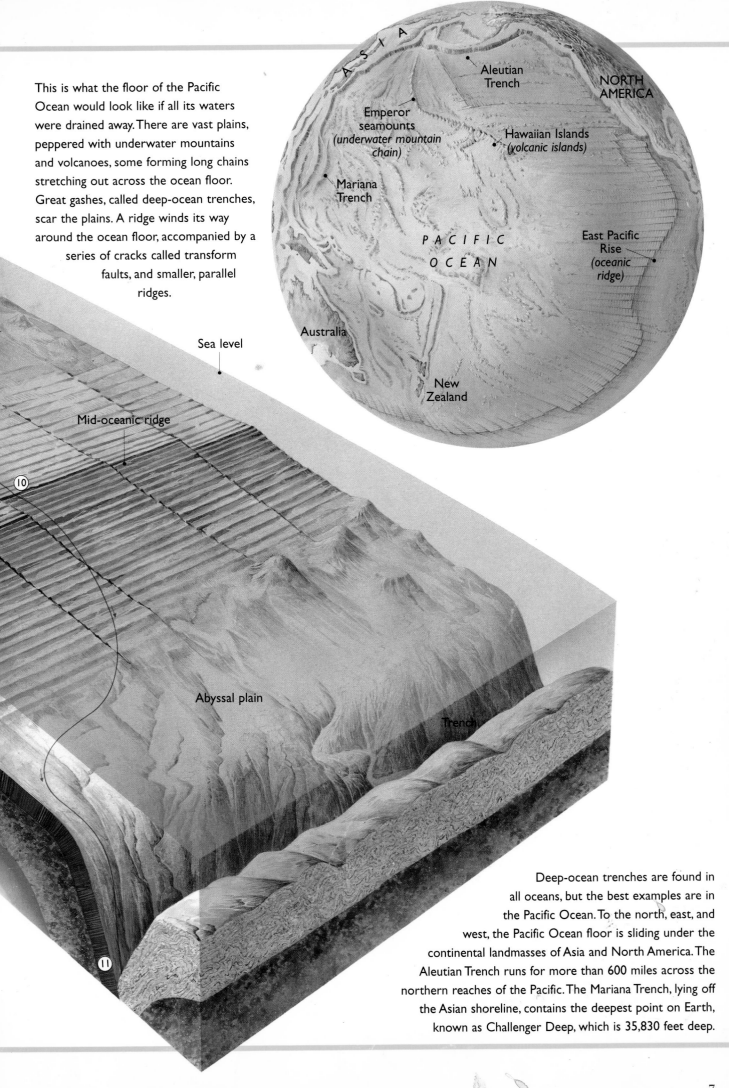

This is what the floor of the Pacific Ocean would look like if all its waters were drained away. There are vast plains, peppered with underwater mountains and volcanoes, some forming long chains stretching out across the ocean floor. Great gashes, called deep-ocean trenches, scar the plains. A ridge winds its way around the ocean floor, accompanied by a series of cracks called transform faults, and smaller, parallel ridges.

A S I A

Aleutian Trench

NORTH AMERICA

Emperor seamounts (underwater mountain chain)

Hawaiian Islands (volcanic islands)

Mariana Trench

East Pacific Rise (oceanic ridge)

P A C I F I C
O C E A N

Australia

New Zealand

Sea level

Mid-oceanic ridge

10

Abyssal plain

Trench

11

Deep-ocean trenches are found in all oceans, but the best examples are in the Pacific Ocean. To the north, east, and west, the Pacific Ocean floor is sliding under the continental landmasses of Asia and North America. The Aleutian Trench runs for more than 600 miles across the northern reaches of the Pacific. The Mariana Trench, lying off the Asian shoreline, contains the deepest point on Earth, known as Challenger Deep, which is 35,830 feet deep.

Seashore

OUR JOURNEY to the bottom of the ocean begins at the seashore, the place where land meets sea. A seashore may consist of rocky cliffs, a sandy or pebble beach, or mudflats bordering a river mouth or estuary. It is often a mixture of all three kinds.

The animals that live on the seashore must be able to withstand the power of waves crashing against the rocks or on to the beach. Limpets, for example, grip the rock so tightly that even the mightiest waves cannot shift them. Barnacles are actually cemented to the rocks. Sand-dwellers, like crabs and worms, burrow under the sand—also a way to avoid being preyed upon by seabirds.

Because of the tides, all seashore animals and plants must be able to live at least part of their lives out of the water. Some animals, including sea anemones and starfish, need to be submerged most of the time, but shelled animals such as limpets, mussels, and periwinkles, can live further out of the water. Their tight shells can keep in the vital moisture for several hours.

Seawater may be contained between rocks to form rock pools. The pools are often rich in marine life, including seaweed, fish, prawns, starfish, sea anemones, and hermit crabs (so-called because they have adopted a shell left by a dead shelled animal). The rock pools may become very warm in hot sunshine or suddenly flooded at high tide. Only certain animals can survive these changing conditions.

TIDES

Sea levels rise and fall usually twice a day, a pattern known as the tides. They are due to gravity: the force of attraction that a large body can exert over something else—in this case, the Moon on the Earth's oceans. As the Earth spins, the waters on that side of the Earth closest to the Moon (and the opposite side) bulge outwards, resulting in higher sea levels, known as high tide. Low tide is reached when that side of the Earth is at right angles to the Moon.

When the Moon and Sun are in line their combined gravitational pull produces the greatest extremes of high

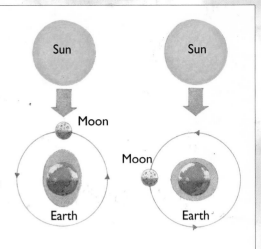

and low tides, known as spring tides *(above left)*. The extremes are at their lowest when the Sun and Moon are pulling at right angles to each other: a neap tide *(above right)*.

KELP FOREST

TRAVELING a short way out to sea we come across a great underwater forest. Giant, leafy "trees" more than 130 feet high sway in the water. The forest is alive with many different animals gliding or creeping about in search of their prey.

These "trees" are not real trees, of course, but a kind of seaweed called giant kelp. Kelp soaks up nutrients from the water around it, so it has no need of roots. Instead, it has a claw-shaped foot, called a holdfast, that anchors it firmly to the sea bed. Occasionally ripped apart in storms, kelp can grow back as quickly as 20 inches a day. It must reach the sunlight at the surface—essential for its survival.

A number of animals graze on the thick, rubbery kelp. They include some kinds of sea snail and sea urchin. These animals can chew right through the stems, leaving the giant kelp to drift away in the tide. It is the torn-off fragments of kelp that provide most animals of the kelp forest with their bountiful food supply. Fish, sponges, sea anemones, worms, starfish, octopuses, sea slugs, and crabs live well on this diet, while they, in turn, are prey for larger fish and mammals such as sea lions and otters.

KEY

1 California sea lion
2 Sea otter
3 Kelp
4 Harbor seal
5 Greenling
6 Giant kelp fish
7 Garibaldi
8 Spiny lobster
9 Brittle star
10 Starfish
11 Blacksmith
12 Sheepshead
13 Sea urchins
14 Scorpion fish
15 Sea snail

URCHIN EATERS

Sea otters live in the kelp forests off the west coast of North America and the northeast coast of Russia. They keep down the numbers of kelp-eating sea urchins by eating them. The otters are experts at breaking open the urchins' spiny shells to feed on the soft insides. Floating on their backs, they crack open urchins (wrapped in a piece of kelp for easy handling) by beating them against a large, flat stone placed on their belly. Sea otters spend the night safely wrapped up in the kelp, to stop them drifting out to sea. To keep warm in the cold water, they must keep active, filling their fur with bubbles that help to prevent heat loss.

ABOVE THE WAVES

THE FIRST LAYER of the ocean we visit is the air just above its surface. This is not just the domain of birds. A number of ocean animals sometimes temporarily leave their watery home for the air above. Flying fish frequently skim the surface of the water, gliding for distances of up to 300 feet or so. Their "wings" are actually long, taut fins. They "fly" to escape predators in the water, but they risk being taken in mid-air by birds.

Many whales and dolphins leap out of the water, a feat known as breaching. Some smaller species can go very high and often perform somersaults while they are in the air.

Just as ocean animals leap clear of the water, so birds sometimes descend into the ocean to catch food. The tropic bird and booby actually plunge into the water, while others, such as the albatross, take fish from the surface with their beak or claws. Air trapped in the feathers of diving birds enables them to rise to the surface quickly and fly away with their catch.

A few creatures live half above and half below the water. The upper part of a Portuguese man-of-war consists of an air sac, giving it buoyancy. Carried by the wind and currents, its stinging tentacles trail in the water, trapping small fish.

KEY

1 Magnificent frigatebird
2 Red-tailed tropic bird
3 Portuguese man-of-war
4 Wandering albatross
5 Bottlenose dolphin
6 Flying fish
7 Brown booby

WAVES

Waves are caused by wind. As air moves across the surface of the ocean, the water turns over and over in circles, forming waves. The water in a wave does not itself move forward: The wave is like a ripple in a shaken rope. Close to shore, the lower part of a wave drags on the sea bed, causing the upper part, the crest, to topple over or "break."

SURFACE WATERS

W E ARE NOW in what some scientists call the "roof" of the ocean, the top 650 feet or so. Here the rays of the sun still penetrate the water and so allow plants to grow. All plants depend on sunlight to enable them to photosynthesize, the way in which they convert carbon dioxide and water into food. The plant life in the open ocean is not like that on land—the plants do not have stems, roots, or leaves. Instead, ocean plants, called phytoplankton, are microscopic in size and float around in the ocean currents, living off the chemical nutrients dissolved in the water.

Microscopic animals, called zooplankton, drift in the surface waters and feed on the phytoplankton. Both kinds of plankton provide food for a wide range of animals, including jellyfish, shrimp, fish, and even huge whales. Other kinds of fish, mammals, turtles, and diving birds prey on some of the plankton-eaters.

The most common kinds of phytoplankton (below, left) are called diatoms. These are very simple life-forms, no bigger than a few thousandths of an inch in size. Seen under a microscope, however, they have beautifully detailed patterns. Delicate "hairs" or whiplike "oars" help keep them floating at or near the water's surface as they drift along in the currents. Zooplankton (below, right) include the larvae (young) of fish, sea anemones, crabs, and krill. The most common kinds of zooplankton are tiny relatives of crabs and shrimps called copepods.

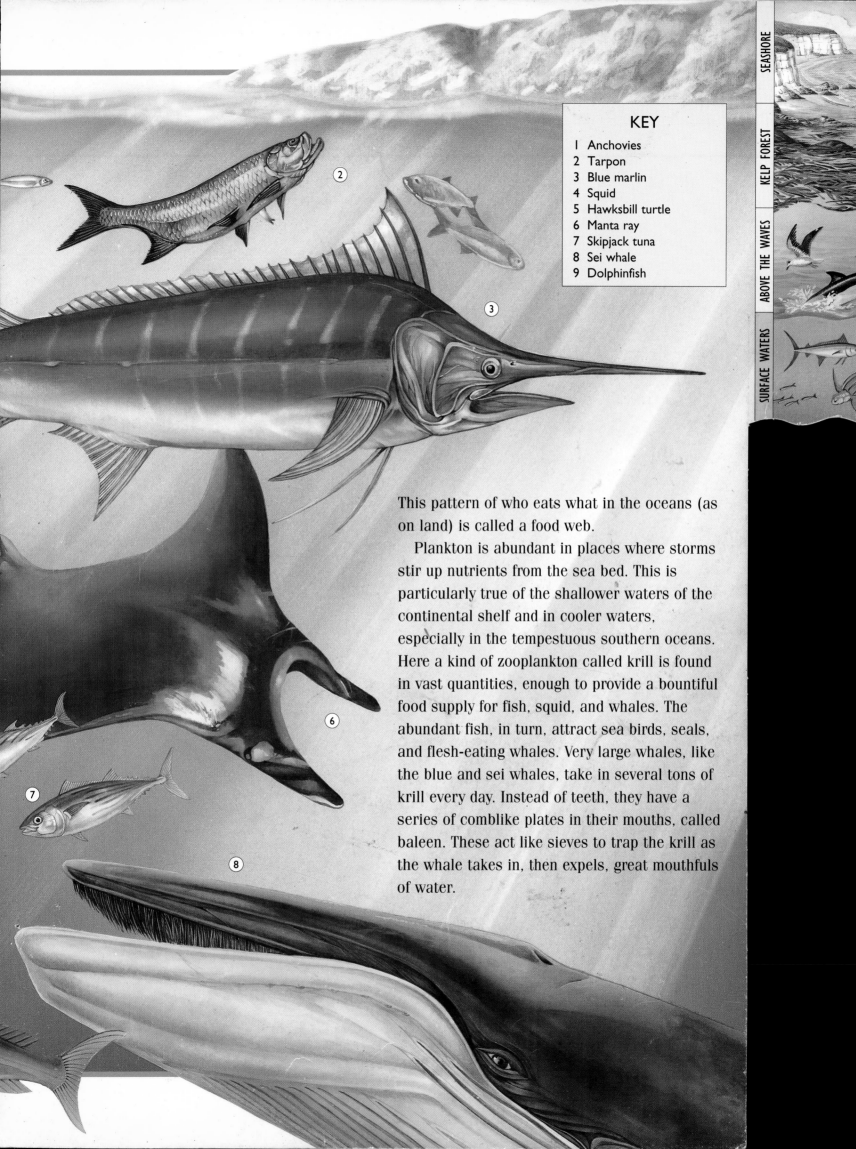

KEY

1 Anchovies
2 Tarpon
3 Blue marlin
4 Squid
5 Hawksbill turtle
6 Manta ray
7 Skipjack tuna
8 Sei whale
9 Dolphinfish

This pattern of who eats what in the oceans (as on land) is called a food web.

Plankton is abundant in places where storms stir up nutrients from the sea bed. This is particularly true of the shallower waters of the continental shelf and in cooler waters, especially in the tempestuous southern oceans. Here a kind of zooplankton called krill is found in vast quantities, enough to provide a bountiful food supply for fish, squid, and whales. The abundant fish, in turn, attract sea birds, seals, and flesh-eating whales. Very large whales, like the blue and sei whales, take in several tons of krill every day. Instead of teeth, they have a series of comblike plates in their mouths, called baleen. These act like sieves to trap the krill as the whale takes in, then expels, great mouthfuls of water.

TWILIGHT ZONE

So-called because of its two slender fins with paddlelike tips, the oarfish is thought to be the true origin of the sea serpent legends. A red "mane" runs the length of its thirty-foot-long, silver-white body, rising to become a macawlike crest on its head.

B ELOW about 650 feet, very little sunlight penetrates the ocean waters, and below 3,300 feet none gets through at all. The layer of water in between these depths is called the mesopelagic, or twilight, zone. Besides the gloomy light, the pressure of the water is much greater than at the surface and the supply of food is very thin.

Animals of the twilight zone feed on waste material raining down from above—dead animals, decaying phytoplankton and droppings, or their fellow inhabitants. To make the most of the few opportunities that come their way, fish need highly sensitive eyes, gaping jaws with long, stabbing teeth to grip their prey firmly, and large stomachs.

Some fish have organs that produce light *(see page 18).* Viperfish use a light on their dorsal (back) fin to lure their prey towards their fang-like teeth. Barracudinas have loosely-hinged jaws and expanding stomachs that allow them to consume prey even larger than themselves.

Some animals travel between surface and twilight zones, feeding in one zone and resting in the other. They include the hatchetfish, which journeys to the surface at night to feed, deadly jellyfish, such as the siphonophore, and certain kinds of shark.

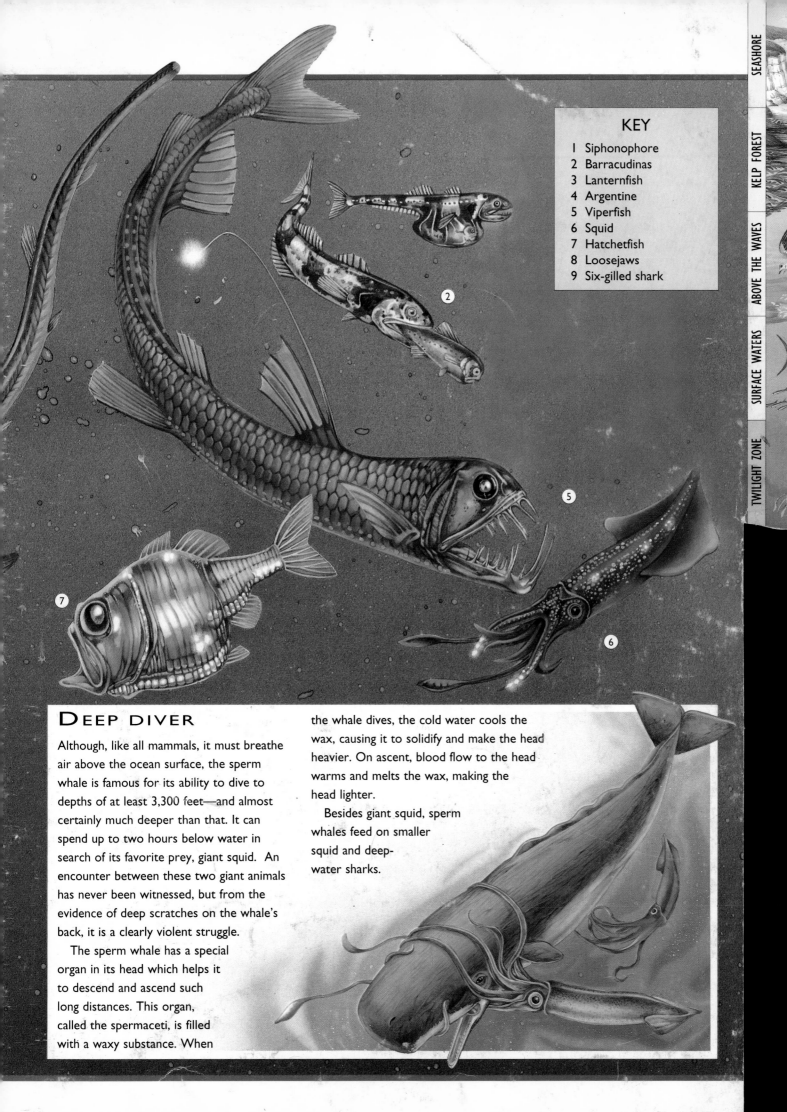

KEY

1 Siphonophore
2 Barracudinas
3 Lanternfish
4 Argentine
5 Viperfish
6 Squid
7 Hatchetfish
8 Loosejaws
9 Six-gilled shark

DEEP DIVER

Although, like all mammals, it must breathe air above the ocean surface, the sperm whale is famous for its ability to dive to depths of at least 3,300 feet—and almost certainly much deeper than that. It can spend up to two hours below water in search of its favorite prey, giant squid. An encounter between these two giant animals has never been witnessed, but from the evidence of deep scratches on the whale's back, it is a clearly violent struggle.

The sperm whale has a special organ in its head which helps it to descend and ascend such long distances. This organ, called the spermaceti, is filled with a waxy substance. When the whale dives, the cold water cools the wax, causing it to solidify and make the head heavier. On ascent, blood flow to the head warms and melts the wax, making the head lighter.

Besides giant squid, sperm whales feed on smaller squid and deep-water sharks.

BATHYPELAGIC ZONE

When some kinds of deep-sea anglerfish mate, the male attaches himself to the female with his jaws, and the two bodies actually fuse together. The eggs float to the surface, where the larvae hatch out.

DEEPER STILL, and below 3,300 feet we enter the near-freezing world of the bathypelagic zone. Even in these completely black, cold depths there is animal life, although it is extremely sparse.

No sunlight at all reaches these parts, yet there is not the total blackness you might expect to find here. Instead of sunlight, it is the animals themselves that provide the light, a feature known as bioluminescence. Fish, squid, jellyfish, and even tiny deep-sea copepods *(see page 8)* all produce their own light. Their light-producing organs have a number of purposes. They may lure prey, act as signals for creatures of the same species, be used as search beams, or help to provide camouflage by "blinding" predators.

Members of the grotesque deep-sea anglerfish family are so-called because of

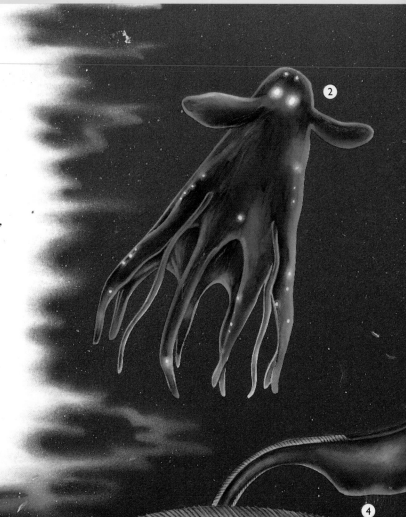

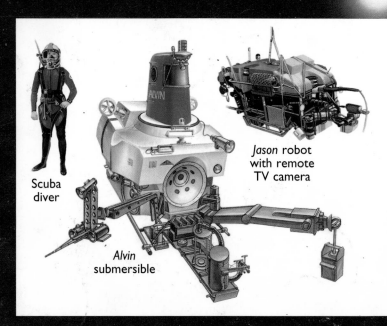

Scuba diver

Jason robot with remote TV camera

Alvin submersible

EXPLORING THE DEEP

It is not possible for humans to swim to any great depth. The problem is the enormous pressure. (A polystyrene cup taken to the bottom of the ocean would come back 10 times smaller, because the tiny air bubbles would have been crushed on all sides. The effect on a human being might be similar!) Scuba divers do not usually go deeper than 160 feet. Below this depth, the pressure causes the air in their breathing apparatus to become too concentrated. Submersibles with thick metal walls strong enough to withstand enormous pressure allow people to travel much deeper. Alternatively, robot cameras can allow us a clear view of life thousands of feet below the ocean surface.

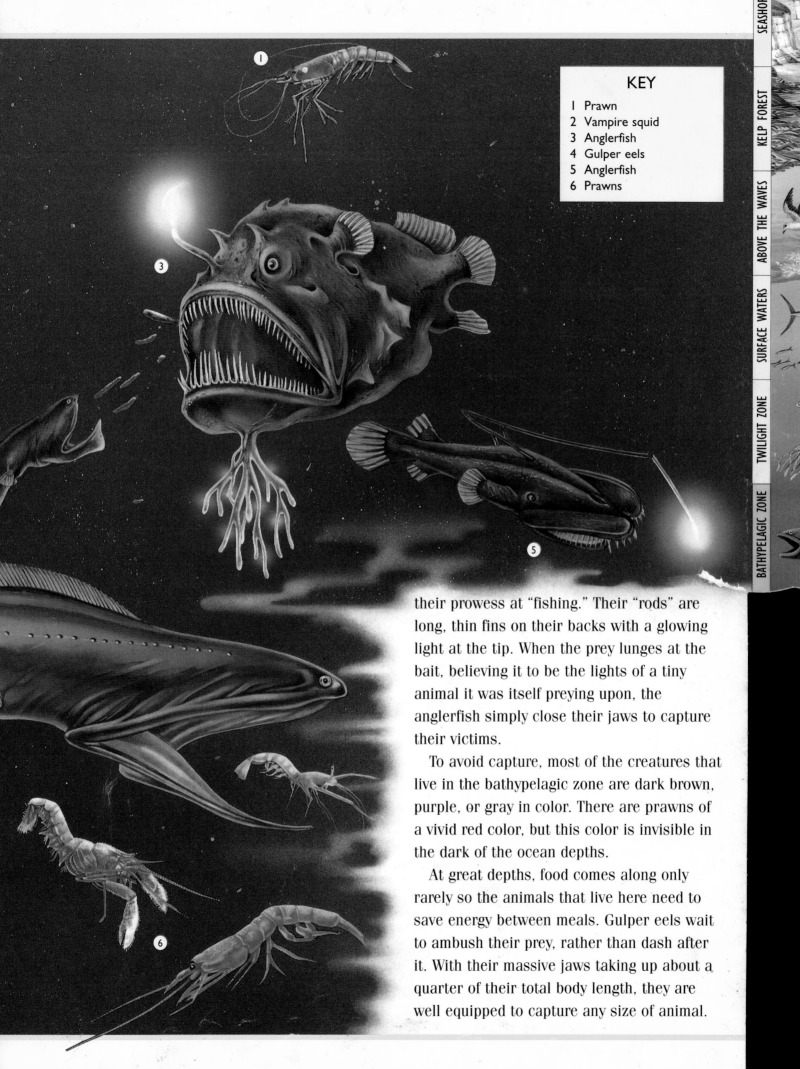

SEASHORE

KELP FOREST

ABOVE THE WAVES

SURFACE WATERS

TWILIGHT ZONE

BATHYPELAGIC ZONE

KEY

1 Prawn
2 Vampire squid
3 Anglerfish
4 Gulper eels
5 Anglerfish
6 Prawns

their prowess at "fishing." Their "rods" are long, thin fins on their backs with a glowing light at the tip. When the prey lunges at the bait, believing it to be the lights of a tiny animal it was itself preying upon, the anglerfish simply close their jaws to capture their victims.

To avoid capture, most of the creatures that live in the bathypelagic zone are dark brown, purple, or gray in color. There are prawns of a vivid red color, but this color is invisible in the dark of the ocean depths.

At great depths, food comes along only rarely so the animals that live here need to save energy between meals. Gulper eels wait to ambush their prey, rather than dash after it. With their massive jaws taking up about a quarter of their total body length, they are well equipped to capture any size of animal.

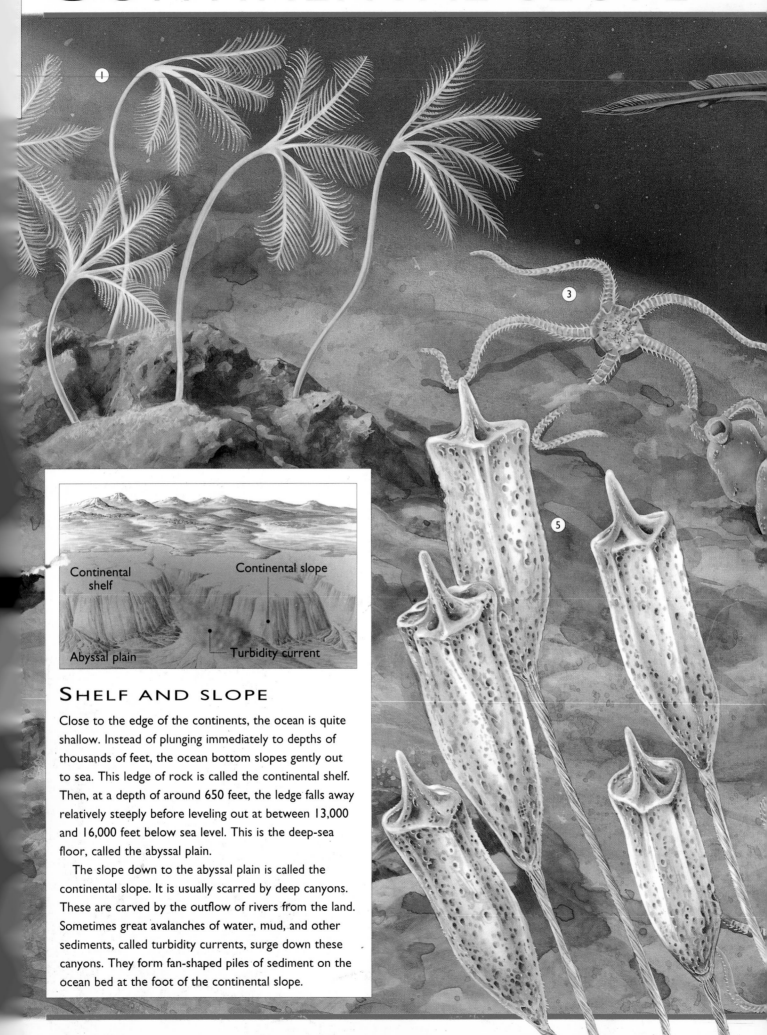

Continental
shelf

Continental slope

Abyssal plain

Turbidity current

SHELF AND SLOPE

Close to the edge of the continents, the ocean is quite
shallow. Instead of plunging immediately to depths of
thousands of feet, the ocean bottom slopes gently out
to sea. This ledge of rock is called the continental shelf.
Then, at a depth of around 650 feet, the ledge falls away
relatively steeply before leveling out at between 13,000
and 16,000 feet below sea level. This is the deep-sea
floor, called the abyssal plain.

The slope down to the abyssal plain is called the
continental slope. It is usually scarred by deep canyons.
These are carved by the outflow of rivers from the land.
Sometimes great avalanches of water, mud, and other
sediments, called turbidity currents, surge down these
canyons. They form fan-shaped piles of sediment on the
ocean bed at the foot of the continental slope.

SEASHORE

KELP FOREST

ABOVE THE WAVES

SURFACE WATERS

TWILIGHT ZONE

BATHYPELAGIC ZONE

CONTINENTAL SLOPE

A T LAST, at a depth of about 8,000 feet, we have finally reached the ocean bed. We touch down on the continental slope, the edge that leads down from the continental shelf to the abyssal plain.

The constant rain of decomposed animal and plant material from the surface waters has settled on the rocky bottom to form a soft, muddy "ooze." Unlike the bathypelagic zone where life-forms are relatively sparse, there are plenty of animals hunting and scavenging for food. Some sieve food particles from the water or simply eat the ooze. The batfish crawls over the ocean bed feeding on bottom-living animals. A kind of lobster with its tail folded under its body, called a squat lobster, also creeps over the soft mud.

Some animals remain in one spot. Among them are sponges, including some that look quite similar to white tropical flowers on long stalks. There are also sea squirts, like bags of living jello, and stalked crinoids, their ribbonlike tentacles (which sieve food particles from the water) wafting in the current.

21

ABYSSAL PLAIN

WE HAVE NOW arrived on the flattest, most featureless, least explored place on Earth: the abyssal plain. We will come across mountains, ridges, and trenches as we cross the plain, but for the most part it is nothing more than a vast, flat field of muddy ooze.

The animals that live out their lives on the abyssal plain must either lift themselves clear of the mud, burrow inside it, or find some way of slithering across it. Sea pens look like plants: They have thin stalks anchored in the mud, with crowns of tentacles that catch their prey. Venus flower baskets, a type of sponge, look like long vases made of woven strands of glass. Tripodfish, as their name suggests, perch on their stiltlike fins above the muddy bed. They keep their front fins outspread to detect passing prey—a bright red deep-sea prawn, for example. When something comes within reach, the tripodfish pushes forward to take it in its mouth.

Worms burrow into the ooze. Patterns made in the bed by these worms last a long time in the still waters, as do the trails made by sea cucumbers. So-called because of the shape of their soft bodies, sea cucumbers crawl slowly about, feeding on the animal or plant remains in the ooze. There are several different kinds: Some have short peglike legs and spikes on their backs, while others have strange "sails." Sea spiders, some of them giants over a foot wide, pick their way across the mud in search of worms to eat.

IN THE OOZE

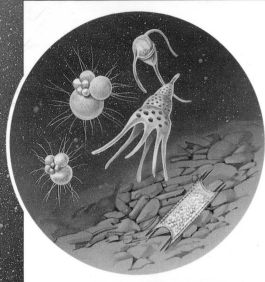

The ocean floor has a rocky bottom, but it is carpeted by ooze—a layer of sediments up to about 1,500 feet thick in places. Sediments are very small fragments of rock such as gravel, sand, or mud. Ocean sediments have taken millions of years to accumulate. A good part of ocean-floor ooze is made up from the skeletons of tiny plankton *(left)* that have rained slowly down from surface waters.

KEY

1 Rat-tail
2 Sea pen
3 Prawn
4 Sea cucumber
5 Tripodfish
6 Sea cucumber
7 Venus flower baskets
8 Sea spider
9 Sea cucumber
10 Sea pens
11 Sea urchin

SEASHORE

KELP FOREST

ABOVE THE WAVES

SURFACE WATERS

TWILIGHT ZONE

BATHYPELAGIC ZONE

CONTINENTAL SLOPE

ABYSSAL PLAIN

CORAL REEF

The Great Barrier Reef runs for more than 1,200 miles along the northeastern coast of Australia. It is the world's largest coral reef, and the largest structure made by living things. It was even visible to astronauts standing on the Moon nearly 250,000 miles away! Actually a string of 2,500 separate reefs towering 400 ft above the sea bed, it measures up to 90 miles across in places. Between 200 and 350 kinds of coral are found there.

Many coral reefs around the world are under threat. Polluted waters, damage from tourism, dredging for shipping lanes, and collection for jewelry all destroy coral that has been growing for many millions of years.

The clownfish (above) lives among the poisonous tentacles of sea anemones on the coral reef. The fish itself is protected from the poison, but its enemies would be stung to death.

FROM THE DEPTHS of the abyssal plain, we are now traveling upwards. We have come across an undersea volcano and are ascending its steep slopes. Several feet before we reach the ocean surface, we are greeted by an amazing sight—coral, in many beautiful shapes and colors, together with an incredible variety of fish and other marine life.

The ocean floor has thousands of such volcanoes, which occur in places where hot, molten rock called magma rises through cracks in the Earth's crust. The magma cools quickly in the cold water, but repeated eruptions cause the volcano to grow bigger and bigger. Some volcanoes break the surface of the ocean and form islands. From its base on the ocean floor to the tip of its summit, Mauna Kea on the Pacific island of Hawaii rises 33,470 feet—the tallest mountain in the world.

AN ATOLL FORMS

When hot magma stops rising through it, a volcano will sink back into the ocean floor. If it does so quite slowly—at a rate less than 0.3 inches per year—the coral continues to grow upwards, forming a circular barrier reef and enclosing a lagoon around the dwindling island. Eventually, the volcanic island disappears, leaving a ring of coral islands called an atoll. Many islands in the South Pacific Ocean are atolls.

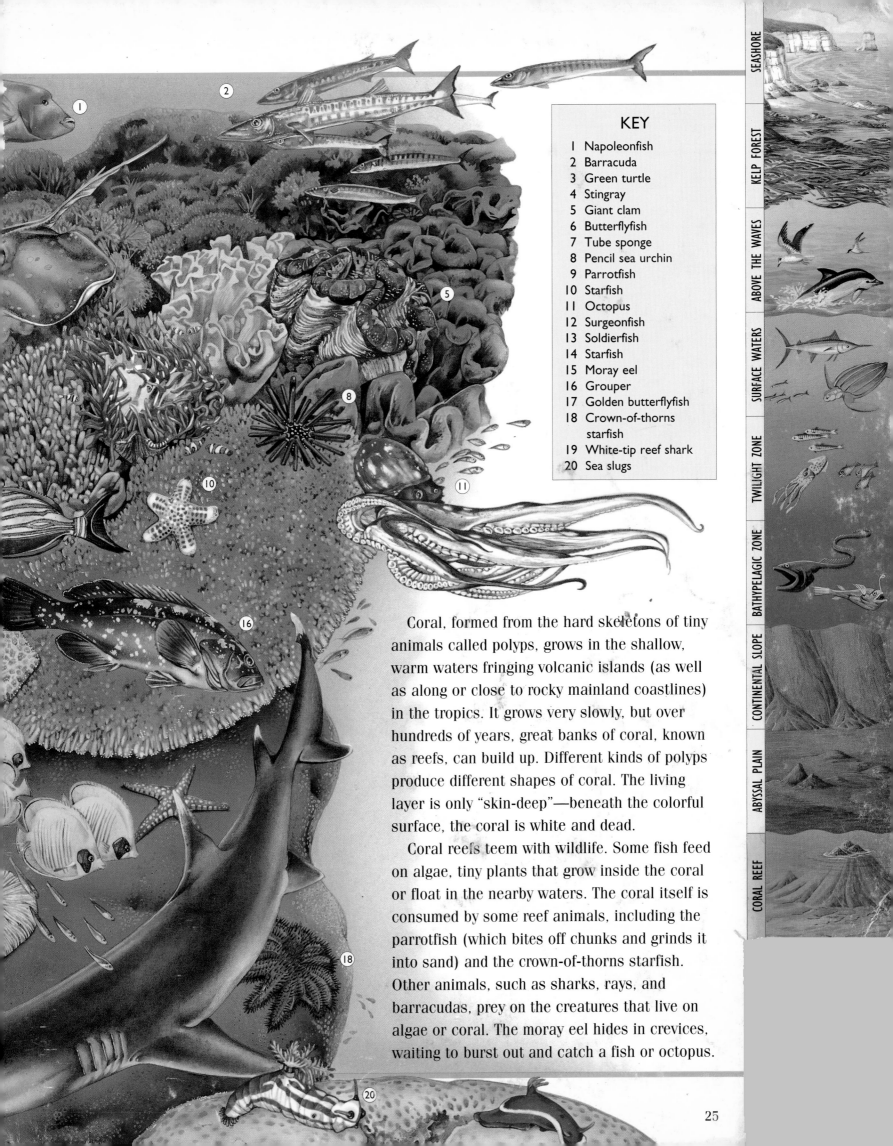

SEASHORE

KELP FOREST

ABOVE THE WAVES

SURFACE WATERS

TWILIGHT ZONE

BATHYPELAGIC ZONE

CONTINENTAL SLOPE

ABYSSAL PLAIN

CORAL REEF

KEY

1 Napoleonfish
2 Barracuda
3 Green turtle
4 Stingray
5 Giant clam
6 Butterflyfish
7 Tube sponge
8 Pencil sea urchin
9 Parrotfish
10 Starfish
11 Octopus
12 Surgeonfish
13 Soldierfish
14 Starfish
15 Moray eel
16 Grouper
17 Golden butterflyfish
18 Crown-of-thorns
   starfish
19 White-tip reef shark
20 Sea slugs

Coral, formed from the hard skeletons of tiny animals called polyps, grows in the shallow, warm waters fringing volcanic islands (as well as along or close to rocky mainland coastlines) in the tropics. It grows very slowly, but over hundreds of years, great banks of coral, known as reefs, can build up. Different kinds of polyps produce different shapes of coral. The living layer is only "skin-deep"—beneath the colorful surface, the coral is white and dead.

Coral reefs teem with wildlife. Some fish feed on algae, tiny plants that grow inside the coral or float in the nearby waters. The coral itself is consumed by some reef animals, including the parrotfish (which bites off chunks and grinds it into sand) and the crown-of-thorns starfish. Other animals, such as sharks, rays, and barracudas, prey on the creatures that live on algae or coral. The moray eel hides in crevices, waiting to burst out and catch a fish or octopus.

MID-OCEANIC RIDGE

KEY

1 Black smoker
2 Giant tube worms
3 Lobster
4 Giant clams
5 Eelpout
6 Brotulid
7 Crab

The mid-oceanic ridge lies mostly deep beneath oceanic waters. One of the very few places where the ridge does rise above the waves is Iceland in the North Atlantic Ocean. There you can see volcanoes and old lava flows, and track the course of the mid-oceanic ridge across the island.

Hydrothermal vents were discovered only as recently as 1977 by oceanographers working in the submersible *Alvin* near the Galapagos Islands in the Pacific Ocean. Their existence proves that life does not need to depend on sunlight to survive.

Another kind of siphonophore *(see page 16)*, about the size of a ping pong ball, is found near the vents. Nick-named the "dandelion," it is held in place above the sea bed by fine, stinging tentacles. It also uses its tentacles to capture its prey.

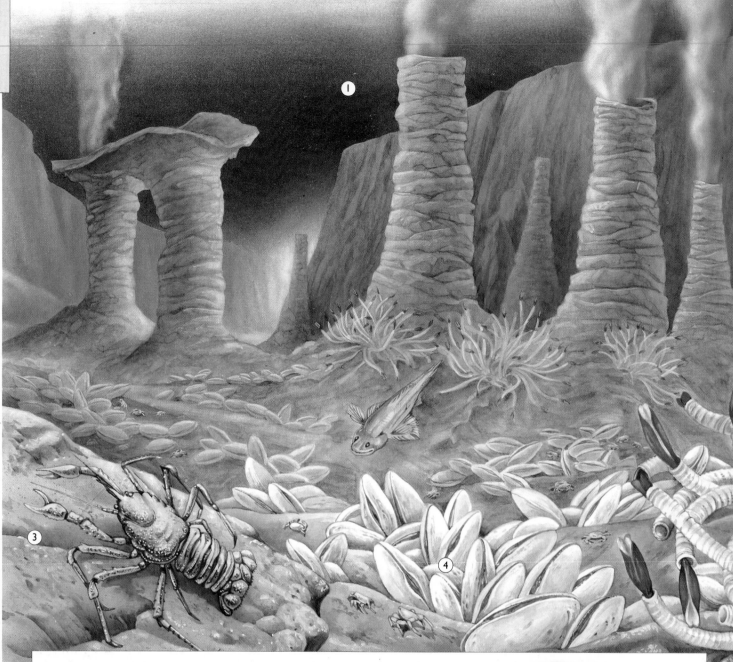

NEW OCEAN FLOOR

All along the mid-oceanic ridge, magma (molten rock) rises from deep inside the Earth. As the magma oozes its way to the surface, the rocks of the old ocean floor are slowly pushed away from the ridge. The magma (now known as lava) erupts from underwater volcanoes before spreading

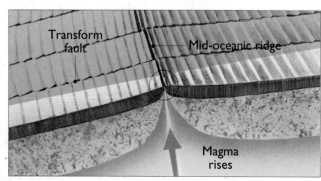

Transform fault

Mid-oceanic ridge

Magma rises

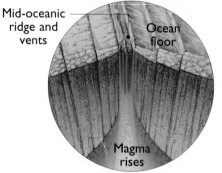

Mid-oceanic ridge and vents

Ocean floor

Magma rises

out, cooling rapidly and solidifying in the cold water. It now forms a new part of the ocean floor. As this process repeats itself, a new ocean floor is gradually formed.

A mid-oceanic ridge is actually made up of a series of smaller ridges, each separated by cracks running at right angles to them. These are called transform faults.

A S WE TRAVEL once more across the abyssal plain, the ground starts to rise and rocky ridges and chasms appear. We are ascending the mid-oceanic ridge. This is a long, undersea mountain chain that snakes all the way around the Earth. It is formed from hot lava erupting from beneath the Earth's crust and cooling *(see panel)*.

Occurring in certain places along the mid-oceanic ridges are cracks in the sea bed through which extremely hot water spurts out. Scientists call these cracks hydrothermal vents. Water that has seeped down into the rocks of the ocean floor is heated by hot magma and blasted back up again through the vents, rich with sulfur and other minerals from the Earth's crust. Known as "black smokers," rocky chimneys several feet high build up around the vents.

Incredibly, some animal life flourishes in the warm water near the vents. There are certain kinds of clams, crabs, lobsters, and a fish called an eelpout. The most amazing creatures are ten-foot-long giant tube worms. Their bright red bodies protrude like thin tulips from their white tube shells. All the animals feed either on the bacteria that take nourishment from the sulfur-rich waters, or prey on the other, bacteria-eating animals.

SEASHORE

KELP FOREST

ABOVE THE WAVES

SURFACE WATERS

TWILIGHT ZONE

BATHYPELAGIC ZONE

CONTINENTAL SLOPE

ABYSSAL PLAIN

CORAL REEF

MID-OCEANIC RIDGE

DEEP-OCEAN TRENCH

In 1960 two scientists, Jacques Piccard and Don Walsh, descended in a bathyscaphe (a kind of submersible) named *Trieste*, almost to the deepest point on Earth: Challenger Deep in the Mariana Trench in the Pacific Ocean. In a dive lasting nearly five hours, they reached a depth of 35,800 feet. Piccard and Walsh made the journey in an observation capsule attached to the underside of *Trieste*. To withstand the enormous pressure, the capsule walls were about 5 inches thick.

As fast as a new ocean floor is being created at the mid-oceanic ridge *(see page 26)*, the old ocean floor near the margins of the continents is being swallowed up in the Earth's depths. What makes the tectonic plates, which make up the outer layer of the Earth, move about, causing this "life-cycle" for the ocean floor? The answer is circular flows of heat through the mantle, an inner layer of the Earth. The plates ride like rafts on slow-moving, partially-molten rock inside the Earth.

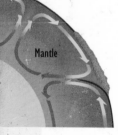

Mantle

This illustration *(right)* shows part of the Mariana Trench, the deepest of all. For comparison, here is also an illustration of one of the tallest buildings in the world, the Empire State Building, which is 1,473 feet high.

WE HAVE DESCENDED back to the abyssal plain, but soon we find ourselves diving even further, plunging mile after mile downwards. We are now in a deep-ocean trench, one of the deepest points on Earth.

Oceanographers call this part of the ocean floor the "hadal zone" (after Hades, the Greek god of the underworld). Animals have even been found to live at these incredible depths, between 20,000 and 30,000 feet. They are so well-adapted to living in such high-pressure conditions—their bodies have no air spaces inside them—that they would die if they were moved to shallower, lower-pressure waters. The ocean bed at the bottom of a trench is flat and covered with ooze. Certain kinds of sea cucumber live here as well as polychaete (pronounced "polly-keet") worms, animals with fleshy "legs" and bristles. There is a kind of sea anemone consisting of a crown of tentacles and a slimy tube. The anemone slips down into the mud to escape predators. The world's deepest-living fish, called brotulids, are also known to inhabit these depths.

Empire State Building

10,000 ft

13,000 ft

16,000 ft

20,000 ft

23,000 ft

26,000 ft

29,000 ft

30,000 ft

KEY
1 Brotulid
2 Sea anemone
3 Sea cucumber
4 Polychaete worm

Trench

Volcano

Continental plate

Oceanic plate

Molten rock

MOVING PLATES

A deep-ocean trench forms where the ocean floor is slowly sliding down into the Earth. This happens when two great slabs making up the Earth's outer shell, called tectonic plates, push together. A plate that is made up of a landmass or continent will ride over the top of one consisting of the heavier ocean floor. The downward movement of the oceanic plate is called subduction. The subducting ocean floor results in a deep trench. Trenches occur all round the Pacific Ocean. As the ocean floor sinks into the Earth, it melts in the great heat. The molten rock, containing the wet sediments from the ocean floor, finds its way up through the continental rocks, erupting at the surface in volcanoes. That is why the area surrounding the Pacific Ocean is often called the "Ring of Fire."

SEASHORE

KELP FOREST

ABOVE THE WAVES

SURFACE WATERS

TWILIGHT ZONE

BATHYPELAGIC ZONE

CONTINENTAL SLOPE

ABYSSAL PLAIN

CORAL REEF

MID-OCEANIC RIDGE

OCEAN TRENCH

GLOSSARY

Abyssal plain A large, flat region of the ocean floor lying mainly between 13,000 and 16,000 feet below the ocean surface. Covered by a thick layer of mud and other sediments, it forms about 40% of the Earth's surface.

Bathypelagic zone The layer of ocean water where no sunlight penetrates—below about 3,300 feet, but excluding the layer of water immediately above the abyssal plain.

Bioluminescence The production of light by living things. It enables deep-ocean animals to locate one another for mating, or to attract their prey.

Continental shelf That part of the continental landmass that lies under ocean waters. Lying no deeper than 650 feet below the surface, the continental shelf produces a narrow area of shallow water surrounding each continent.

Continental slope Part of the ocean floor that leads from the edge of the continental shelf down to the abyssal plain.

Coral A hard substance produced by tiny animals called polyps. These animals, which often live in large colonies, build up a stony skeleton—the coral—around themselves. When they die, new polyps grow in their remains and add to the coral. Over time, a coral reef is built up.

Deep-ocean trench A long, very deep valley in the sea bed, plunging to depths of between 20,000 and 30,000 feet.

Food web In a food chain, a plant, for example, is eaten by an animal, which is eaten by another animal, and so on. A food web describes a more complicated pattern in which plants and animals living in the same environment depend on each other for their food.

Hydrothermal vent A crack in the sea bed found in certain places on mid-oceanic ridges where very hot, sulfur-rich water is released from the rocks below.

Lava Magma that has erupted at the Earth's surface through volcanoes.

Magma Hot, molten rock formed in the upper mantle, the layer of the Earth lying beneath its outer layer, the crust.

Mid-oceanic ridge A long mountain range running along the ocean floor, formed where lava erupts along a boundary between two tectonic plates.

Nutrients Vital chemical substances needed by all living things to enable them to live and grow.

Ooze A layer of mud and other sediments on the sea floor. It may lie up to 1,500 feet thick in places.

Photosynthesis The process by which plants use sunlight as an energy source to turn carbon dioxide and water into the sugars they need for food.

Plankton The microscopic plants and animals that drift in vast numbers chiefly in the surface waters of the ocean. They form a vital part of the oceanic food web. Phyto-plankton (plants) include simple life-forms such as diatoms. Zooplankton (animals) include the young of a huge number of animal types, as well as many other tiny creatures such as copepods.

Pressure The force exerted by something on a certain area or surface. In the oceans, pressure increases with depth and acts in all directions. At a depth of 30,000 feet, the pressure of water is about the same as that exerted by seven elephants standing on a saucer!

Seamount A mountain, volcanic in origin, that rises 3,300 feet or more from the sea floor but remains wholly submerged.

Sediment Fragments of rock that have been deposited by water, wind, or ice. Gravel, sand, mud, and the remains of living things are all kinds of sediment.

Subduction The process by which the edge of one tectonic plate slides down beneath another, producing a deep-ocean trench.

Submersible An underwater vessel, much smaller than a submarine, that is maneuverable and carries passengers.

Tectonic plates The large slabs into which the surface of the Earth is divided. Tectonic plates gradually move relative to each another, sometimes colliding, sometimes moving apart. Beneath the oceans, colliding plates result in subduction, while plates moving apart produce the mid-oceanic ridge.

Twilight zone The layer of ocean water between 650 and 3,300 feet below the surface, where very little sunlight penetrates through from above.

Volcano Any opening in the Earth's crust through which lava erupts. The name is often used to describe a cone-shaped mountain with a central vent for the erupting lava, but the cracks or fissures along mid-oceanic ridges are also kinds of volcanoes.

FURTHER READING

Cooper, Ann. *Along the Seashore.* Roberts Rinehart, 1997.

Cross, Kathy. *Crafts for Kids Who Are Wild About Oceans.* Millbrook Press, 1998.

Earle, Sylvia A. *Dive: My Adventures in the Deep Frontier.* National Geographic Society, 1999.

Fredericks, Anthony D., et al. *Exploring the Oceans: Science Activities for Kids.* Fulcrum, 1998.

Gibbons, Gail. *Exploring the Deep, Dark Sea.* Little, Brown & Co., 1999.

Lambert, David. *The Kingfisher Young People's Book of Oceans.* Kingfisher Books, 1997.

Nye, Bill. *Bill Nye the Science Guy's Big Blue Ocean.* Disney Press, 1999.

Simon, Seymour. *Oceans.* Mulberry Books, 1997.

Wu, Norbert. *Beneath the Waves: Exploring the Hidden World of the Kelp Forest.* Chronicle Books, 1997.